I Saw A Dragonfly

I Saw A Dragonfly

Gregory L. Idleman

iUniverse, Inc.
New York Lincoln Shanghai

I Saw A Dragonfly

iUniverse books may be ordered through booksellers or by contacting:

iUniverse
2021 Pine Lake Road, Suite 100
Lincoln, NE 68512
www.iuniverse.com
1-800-Authors (1-800-288-4677)

Because of the dynamic nature of the Internet, any Web addresses or links contained in this book may have changed since publication and may no longer be valid.

The views expressed in this work are solely those of the author and do not necessarily reflect the views of the publisher, and the publisher hereby disclaims any responsibility for them.

ISBN: 978-0-595-46390-9 (pbk)
ISBN: 978-0-595-90683-3 (ebk)

Printed in the United States of America

Contents

Preface

This is a moving, real-life, love story about a middle aged couple's struggle with a terminal illness, the passing of the wife, and the subsequent grieving of the husband. Cindy and Greg Idleman lived in a small, rural community in east, central Illinois. Having been the love of one another's lives, the bond between them has never broken, even after Cindy's passing. Emotional, but glorious stories are contained within that will assuredly strengthen your faith in the Lord God almighty.

A tremendous thanks goes out to all that helped Cindy during the last two years of her life. It is testament that when one lives their life spreading God's love, that it indeed shall come to reward you. A special thank you to the dear friends that assisted in the editing of this book.

For those that have lost a loved one, may this give you hope and strength. Those that are grieving, may these words help you to get things in proper perspective and see life again. God bless you all and may his word lead you through your own personal journey.

Greg Idleman

1

"The Beginning"

It was Friday, March 13, 1992, snow lightly covered the ground, as Cindy and I, and her four children drove to a friends log home where we were to be wed at 6:00 PM. All nervous of the life changing event that was to take place shortly, it was the happiest of times; a time of new beginning.

Cindy and I both grew up in the small east central Illinois town of Paris only two blocks from one another. Although she was three years older, we casually knew one another through our grandparents and Cindy's father worked with my great aunt who was raising my older brother and me. Cindy's childhood was quite traumatic as her father contracted polio when she was three years old. It was a full time job for Mary Ann, Cindy's mother, just caring for Rusty, her father, as he battled daily to survive with post-polio syndrome. In the early stages of the disease Rusty was rushed out of state to live in an iron lung for several months, followed by months of rehabilitation learning all over again how to do the simplest of everyday tasks. During this time Cindy and her older brother Tim stayed with friends and family. Being a family of quite meager means, lack of finances further added to life's challenges. I reflect back and wonder how Mary Ann ever withstood the pressures.

When Rusty finally returned home, they all tried to live as normal a life as possible, but daily care of Rusty was an enormous task. Most of Mary Ann's time and energy were spent caring for Rusty, Tim had to be the man of the house at a very early age and Cindy, a quite precocious child, was expected to be a well-mannered young lady. In time Rusty improved to the point that he was able to run for election and then serve as the County Clerk for over twenty years. This would not have been possible without the support of the entire family, but life started to fall into place and have normalcy allowing Rusty to provide for his family.

Shortly after high school Cindy married. The marriage was difficult and at times abusive; but, through it all, Cindy became the mother of her dear four children Andy, Ginni, Tim, and Jon. She put her whole life into loving her children and making their life as happy a time as she could being involved in all their activities, working as a floral designer, and quite involved in her church made life fast paced. She was so full of love, but one day Cindy's husband announced he was leaving her.... she was heartbroken. What would she do? With no car, how would she get to work? How could she support her four children on a floral designer's salary? There she was, Andy at Purdue University, Ginni in high school, Tim in the 6th grade, and young Jon in the 3rd grade. Somehow through help from family and friends they found a small house in town to rent, an older used car was acquired, and a dear aunt helped Cindy learn to feed her family on minimal funds. Life got back into somewhat of a routine, but being a single parent with no assistance was so hard. It became easier to let the kids be happy than to fight the battles. Cindy's deep faith pulled her through and kept her going.

She told me of one of her deepest moments during Christmas 1991. Trying to give the children as normal a Christmas as she could, she purchased a tree. While trying to get the tree in the stand, she was cutting off a branch at the bottom with all that she had, a butcher knife, and she cut herself severely. As she sat there crying, she was at an all time low in her life. "Why is this happening, everything is a battle, the rent money is all I have to buy any kinds of gifts, and I can't even put up my tree."

We talked about this time in Cindy's life occasionally, the battles she had to fight with family, bill collectors; ... the list goes on and on. I still today so admire her for never giving up, but get absolutely livid with those that hurt my dear Cynthia. So sensitive, kind, and loving, Cindy wore her emotions on her sleeve and all through our marriage I was committed to being her protector. She had endured enough unhappiness already in her life and I was driven to ensure that she would never be hurt again. Of course through the years there were more times of hurt that I could not stop, but hoped to ease the pain and, if needed, to confront those that had hurt her. I have usually been easy going, but when you hurt the one person in my life that loved me as she did, the horns come out. With good reason, Mary Ann called Cindy her little watering pot, as she would cry so easily.

My childhood, as Cindy's, was not always happy and very hard at times. When I was five my mother died in her sleep of severe asthma. I still remember that morning when my brother Wayne and I found her sitting there in her living room chair. We then, with our father, Charles, went to live with my grandmother in an apartment on the second story of her home. My father was a traveling salesman so our grandmother cared for Wayne and me during the week.

Then, one night when I was 8 years old, as we all waited for my Dad to return home, there was an ambulance that went past the house and an empty feeling overcame us. Shortly thereafter, the phone rang. It was the hospital.... . Daddy had fallen asleep and had a fatal car wreck. Oh my God, not again!!!!!!!!!!

Well, our grandmother, then in her 60's and diabetic, took on the task of raising Wayne and I. A year later though, she got sick. Having only one kidney from a previous surgery due to diabetes, her only remaining kidney became infected. The last night home before the ambulance came was, and still is, quite vivid. A few days later, she passed.

Wayne and I once again moved and went to live with our great aunt and uncle on our father's side. They never had children of their own and so in a way my brother and I were the answer to my aunt's prayers, but not so for my uncle. Before we went to live with them, Wayne and I had always enjoyed them. They spoiled us terribly and we loved it. Well, living with them was quite different. Our aunt loved us so much, but it was hard for our uncle, who was angry quite often. As a child, it was not a happy time and lived in constant fear of upsetting him. Today, however, I look back and understand his frustration having his life completely overturned at a later time in their life, when it should have been just he and my aunt to share their golden years. As hard as it was, Wayne and I did not have to go to the Children's Home, which was just across the street, and for that I am eternally grateful.

We lived with our uncle and aunt till I graduated high school. Off to junior college for two years studying Civil Engineering Technology, worked for Illinois DOT in Springfield, then back to college for 4 more years to get a bachelor degree in Civil Engineering from the University of Illinois. I moved back to Paris and went to work again for IDOT as an engineer. During that first summer, my uncle died of a sudden heart attack at home. My aunt, who the day before was driving her girlfriends to all the card parties, was in such shock and mourning that her mind snapped and was never the same. I moved back home to be with her and get her back to normal, but that was not to be. She needed constant care and supervision. A few months later she passed as well.

I continued on with work and purchased their home from the estate. Although Wayne and I lived with them for 14 years, since we were "great" nephews, we were not legally related. Here I lived for several years, spending all my spare time and money heavily involved in drag racing. It was the love of my life, until the IRS decided to take exception to it.

Then, in the winter of 1991 I ran into Cindy again, after many years, at a local flower shop where she was a floral designer. That was the beginning of our whirlwind relationship. Our first date was New Years' Eve and three months later we married. I had never been married before; although I had several relationships but always left with the feeling I cared more for them than they did me. I had been hurt a few times and once really hard, but what a breath of fresh air Cindy was when we started dating. Still today, I can proudly say that "never" had anyone "ever" loved me as Cindy did. I have learned what true love is and it indeed is a very special thing. Cindy was so full of love, making who ever she was with feel special. She loved to laugh and was extremely creative and talented at decorating and floral design, had a beautiful soprano voice, and was indeed an angel here on earth.

So, let the wedding begin. It was small, but very nice and we are forever indebted to our friends that let us be married in their special home. A short honeymoon followed in Nashville, Indiana, our favorite place, and life as Mr. & Mrs. Greg & Cindy Idleman began.

2

"A New Life"

For our honeymoon, Cindy and I spent a few days in Nashville, Indiana, a small town in south western Indiana which originally was noted as an artist colony and now full of various craft shops and small restaurants. The whole town extremely charming and quaint. Most of our time was spent shopping, with Cindy's mission of transforming my little bachelor house into a home decorated in the manner fitting of Cindy. With each new find we became more and more excited to return home and begin the transformation. The decorating was Cindy's job and I turned it all over to her to instill her taste in our new home. I often laugh at husbands that think they should offer their decorating skills and opinions.... how funny.

We returned home with our new treasurers and what a wonderful job Cindy did making our small house into a home she was proud of and a home her four children would enjoy. It was a big change for all of us. I went from living by myself and my two Labradors (Chelsie and Oprah), to having a wife and four children, simply by a simple "I do". It took great adjustments for all and was not always easy. Stepchildren require delicate handling to try and keep peace in the home while having some degree of discipline and respect. I quickly learned to turn the discipline entirely over to Cindy as it caused problems with not only the children, but also between Cindy and me. I loved her with all my heart and was not going to let anything harm that relationship. I would at times be so angry when her children were disrespectful to her, this woman that loved them unconditionally and had stood by them while there father left them all, but if our marriage was to last, I had to keep much of my anger within … it was just not my place to intercede. As the years went by, our lives faced all the challenges that families face, but the experiences helped me to become a fuller and much more understanding person. Cindy was one of those people that had to be involved in what ever was going on. Always eager to lend a hand, volunteer for committee, help a person in need, I followed along and the two of us became quite active in the community. Between both of us working, and attending school events, church activities, civic committees, etc. life was indeed full and busy. Helping Cindy along the way, we made a good team and she trained me to be a fairly good cook, florist, decorator, event planner, choir member, and an all-supporting husband. Although we worked many long hours at our projects, we enjoyed being with one another so much it would have been hard to imagine life any other way. Some couples tend to live separate lives, but not us, we did everything together, supported one another, and had endless respect for each other. This, I think, was the key to the success of our marriage, tremendous respect.

People just loved Cindy. She was fun, upbeat, loved to laugh, and had a gift for making who ever she was with feel special about themselves. Still today, people share Cindy stories of how they met her, what she had done for them that she thought nothing of, but made an unending impression on their lives. She was indeed an angel here on earth. Due to Cindy's soft personality and a hard childhood, she had very low self-esteem and did not realize just how truly gifted she was. She just did what she thought God would have wanted her to do in life and never stopped to think how giving she truly was. I often laughed when she would say she did not have any friends because it could not have been any further from the truth. For the 14 years of our marriage I continually worked to build her up, to help her see what I and her many friends saw.... a fabulous, outgoing, loving person; but she just could not accept how wonderful she really was.

3

"Cindy's Struggle Begins"

Shortly after our marriage, the long string of Cindy's health problems began. I have to believe that things were not well before we married, but being a single parent trying desperately to provide for her children on a florist's salary, she just would not allow her health to stop her.

The second week after we returned home from our honeymoon, one evening I went to a nearby town for a dog show training class with my two Labs. When I returned to Paris, I found that Cindy was in the hospital with Tackacardia (rapid heartbeat). While a scare, they were able to treat it with medication. This was the beginning of a long string of health issues. Through the years Cindy was faced with 2 rotator cuff surgeries, 2 carpal tunnel surgeries, a complete hysterectomy, due to her mother's history of cancer, a complete knee replacement, diabetes, and fibromyalgia. Bless her heart, she put up with all of this while still continuing to work, volunteer, be a wife and mom, and touch the lives of everyone she met.

Then, in the summer of 2004, Cindy starting having more and more issues with exhaustion. She tried to keep involved in life, but her energy level just kept dwindling. We went to the doctor for test after test, after test, and nothing showed up. This went on for a year, frustration building, her energy drained till one day she could barely walk to the doctor's office with my help and was quite disoriented. Not knowing what to do, we were told to take her to the emergency room at a large teaching hospital about an hour away. It was then determined that Cindy problem was her liver.... . finally, an answer. She was diagnosed with Non-Alcoholic Stetohepatitis (NASH), commonly called Fatty Liver Disease. Upon further testing, it was found that it was progressing into Stage 4 liver disease known as Cirrhosis. The only cure would be a liver transplant.

Meeting with the liver specialist, we were optimistic in that finally something had been found and that today liver transplants were very successful. So, we thought, we just needed to get Cindy a new liver. I still remember the day Cindy asked the specialist if she was going to die from this and he said "no". The problem arose in that they would not perform the surgery due to Cindy's weight. Their history had proved that there would be post-surgery complications unless she got to a certain weight. She would need to lose 60 pounds to have the surgery.

We went home with optimism and a plan to start the weight loss. Cindy and I were both very over weight, but lead active lives in spite of it. At home we were faced with two problems, trying to lose weight and managing her blood ammonia level since her liver was not functioning properly. The ammonia level was regulated by a medicine that acted like a strong laxative that she had to take 3 to 4 times a day. It would work for a while, then her stomach would not tolerate it causing pain and vomiting so we would have to stop the medicine. When this happened the ammonia level would skyrocket making here ever so much weaker and would get to the point of making her delirious. She and I spent many scary nights at home until we could not manage and we would go off to the hospital for a few days.

As far as the weight loss, that was a struggle of its own. While Cindy's appetite was minimal, she was not strong enough to walk any appreciable distance without the use of a walker. So, while she ate very little, her metabolism was in starvation mode and the weight came off extremely slow. Finally she got within 25 pounds of where she needed to be and the insurance company approved us to go to St. Louis for a consultation with the liver transplant specialist. I cannot tell you the excitement we felt with the hope that this awful battle would hopefully be coming to an end.

Our trip to St. Louis was a pleasant trip. We were excited, the weather was good, and it seemed our prayers had been answered. We went the night before and stayed at a hotel adjacent to the hospital. The next morning we arose early, got ready and pushed Cindy in her wheelchair over to the hospital. After an anxious wait, we were taken into the surgeon's office. After meeting with the doctor, we did not know whether to cry, be furious, or what. He was the rudest doctor we had ever met, said Cindy was a "terrible" candidate for a liver transplant, needed to lose another 50 pounds and "what was she doing in that wheel chair?" He said come back in 6 months.

We left the hospital in tears. Never had I seen such a rude and uncompassionate display by a doctor. I am an easygoing person, but when you hurt my Cindy, I am out for blood and he had gone too far. He even ask if she was working (obviously looking at her he knew she could not), then ask if she was collecting disability (which she was not), but that was none of his damn business. The trip home was quiet and I spent most of the time trying to console her. There were just no words that would come to me, we both were just crushed.

After we got over the shock of our disastrous St. Louis trip, we met with our local doctor and came up with a new plan. By this time we had gotten pretty good at managing Cindy's ammonia level and as long as her hemoglobin was up (slow internal bleeding), she did pretty well. Still, she needed to use a walker, had to have help bathing, dressing, etc, but was able to get out of bed by herself and use the toilet. As part of our new plan, I took Cindy to physical therapy at the hospital 3 times a week. She worked hard and as long as we kept things regulated, she showed improvement and increased strength.

Then, Cindy started developing problems with ascites. Common in cancer patients, but liver patients as well, it is a collection of fluid in the abdomen that normally would be processed through the liver; but since it had restricted flow; the fluid would go out into her body. When this would happen, her abdomen would be quite distended, caused trouble with breathing and once again zapping her strength. Treatment with diuretics is normal, but in severe cases the fluid has to actually be drained from the body. Just another piece to the puzzle for us to try and manage, but we did what we had to do.

4

"Something Changed"

We got into a routine, trying to manage all Cindy's complications with me trying to continue to go to work, while concentrating on her weight loss and conditioning. Cindy was sleeping a lot during these days due to her exhaustion caused by the liver disease. Each day I would get Cindy's breakfast and medicine before I went to work. During this time she was taking over 20 medications at various times through the day. A little before 8:00 am I would go to work. At 10:00 I would race home to get Cindy up for a bathroom break because she could not get out of bed herself, then hurry back to work. At noon, I would come home for lunch, medicine, and the bathroom. Back to work at 1:00 pm until 3:00 pm and race home again for another bathroom break for Cindy. My workday was over at 4:30 pm. It was good to be at home with my sweetie for the rest of the evening and the rushing was over. That is, except for the 3 days a week we had physical therapy, when I would take leave from work at 3:30 pm, go home, get Cindy up and dressed to head to the hospital. We got into a pretty good routine and thank God for the cooperation and understanding of by supervisor and co-workers.

It was now the first of June 2006. We were doing pretty well, but the ascites was getting worse to the point that the medications were not working and we had to have it drained. The first time they removed 6 liters of fluid and could have done more, but the doctors were afraid to. On June 5, 2006 we were to go to the hospital to have Cindy's hemoglobin checked to see if she needed more blood. Previously, each time she received a transfusion, it really perked her up and we were in hopes of just that. She had gotten quite weak and it indeed appeared to be time again. We put on her housecoat, as she was too exhausted to dress, and using her walker, we went to get in the van. When we got there, to our surprise she was too weak to step into the van and I could not help her enough. So, back to the house we went and it took all the strength she could muster up to get back inside. We sat her in her chair and I called the ambulance. It was our only choice.

Our local emergency services people were truly amazing during all of this and words cannot begin to repay our thanks.

The ambulance came, took Cindy to the emergency room, and she was admitted to the hospital. We both felt after some blood and a check over, we would be home in a day or two. Well, something changed during this stay. Cindy became very weak, nearly unable to stand by herself. Then her bowels stopped working properly which caused her blood ammonia levels to skyrocket. They increased the dosage of medication to evacuate her bowels, but past practice was not working this time. They kept increasing the dosage until she had a bowel movement and each time we thought we were over the hump, but then the bowels would shut down again. The only thing to do was keep after the medication. During these times when her ammonia level would get high, Cindy was nearly comatose, could not speak or was very lucid. Further, her blood sugar was running in the high 300's and no one would increase her insulin. This went on for about a week till we got the ammonia under control.

Then, the weekend from "hell" began. Our normal doctor was leaving town for a few days and another physician was in charge of Cindy. Our doctor, whom we loved very much, left town Friday evening. Saturday morning, Cindy started having bowel problems again and needed a higher dose of her medication to get things flowing. I had been through this many times with Cindy in the past and knew what to do. She was getting worse by the minute and we needed to act. I tried to speak with the weekend doctor, but he would not let me finish a sentence and insisted she was failing and I should call her children and let them know. I cannot tell you how utterly furious I was … furious!!!! The solution was so simple, but he would not listen. I spoke with the nurse and she agreed with the doctor. She spent a lot of time talking to me and had me convinced she was indeed failing fast. I gave in and called the children to let them know what was going on. My heart was broken. This all transpired on a Saturday. I spent the night with Cindy in the hospital; watching her sleep more and more, unable to talk, eat … nothing.

Sunday was a sad day. Cindy's children that lived in the area came to see her, knowing she was not able to communicate, but just to be with her. Then as the day came to an end, a miracle happened. Our regular doctor called in to check on Cindy, found out what was going on and immediately ordered a big increase in her medicine. Thank you Jesus. In a few hours the medicine started to work and she was getting better. I have to tell you that now I have things in life in such a different perspective. There I was, walking the halls of the hospital at 4:00 AM in absolute glee that my wife had just had a bowel movement…. Praise you Jesus!!!!

By Monday morning there was a tremendous improvement in Cindy's condition and she even ate all her breakfast … Amen!!!

The next few days, we kept right after her medicine and she seemed to stabilize. Another draining of the ascites, and we were allowed to go home.

5

"Just A Setback"

On June 16, 2006, one day before Cindy's 54th birthday, we returned home. Cindy rode in the ambulance as we did not want to try getting in the van again and I was glad to have the emergency crews help getting Cindy in the house and settled. Although she was still extremely weak, she was very alert and glad to be home. Truly, I felt we had just had a big setback, but we were both committed to getting her strength back and starting up again with physical therapy.

The 17th was Cindy's birthday and we had a party to plan! The kids all came over and Andy and family made a surprise visit from Massachusetts. It was a good and happy day. Friends stopped by to bring cards and gifts. She thoroughly enjoyed the day. During the first night home, Cindy slept in her recliner as she was afraid to try to make it into the bedroom; but, the night of the 17th we devised a plan where we put chairs along the way (we have a small home mind you) so she could rest as needed while I gave her a bear hug all the way holding her up as we walked. Our plan worked and she got to sleep, finally, in her own bed. Little did I know that it would be her last night for her to ever do that. I had not even thought about that until just now as I write this … oh, how sad.

During all this time I had been in close contact with a nurse working for our health insurance company. She had been assigned Cindy's case from the beginning and is indeed a true angel. She constantly called, sent cards, etc giving us hope and direction on how to proceed with all of this. She is indeed a tribute to her profession. Anyway, I had been updating her on Cindy and she wanted to try to get us help in the home to care better for Cindy and also to help in some way so that I could return to work. It was her suggestion that we sign up with Hospice. The word "Hospice" rang a bell through both our hearts as we had become familiar with the organization a few years back when Cindy's mother was dying of cancer. Although we knew what a wonderful group of people they were, we both thought "that's for terminal patients". The nurse assured us that this was just a way to get us the most in-home help we could get and, when she got better, we could just discontinue. We agreed and signed up with Hospice on June the 18th. It proved to be the right decision. Within the day a Hospice nurse came to assess Cindy, ordered a hospital bed for our living room, oxygen if we needed it, a bedside table, a commode, and all of Cindy's meds. They really got after things and were so thorough. Each day the nurse would check on Cindy and an aide would come bathe her, change her bed, etc. Within a day or two a Hospice social worker came to discuss any problems we may have had and a physical therapist was scheduled. It seemed like things were starting to get back on track.

Cindy was happy at home. We ordered hospital gowns off the Internet in order to make daily bathing easier and to have clean clothes easy to sleep in. The next week I thought I would try to go back to work, with people staying with her when the nurse and aide were not with her. We tried that for part of a day, but it was just not going to work out. Cindy was not resting well, wanted me home, and while at work I worried constantly about her. That afternoon I had a long talk with the Hospice nurse wanting to know in her opinion on what I should do. She said she felt, if I could, I should spend as much time with Cindy as possible. I ask "are you saying.... she is going to die?" Greg, she said, "yes, I can't tell you when, but I can see small changes in her and yes,.... . she is going to die. I do not know if it is going to be weeks or months, but if you can ... spend this time together." Well, that answered my question. I had worked at IDOT for 30 years and had a very large sick leave bank built up. Now was the time to use it and if I ran out, I would worry about that at the time. I spoke with my boss and co-workers telling them what was up and that I would not be back for a while.

There was a relief felt in both of us once this decision was made. Cindy and I had always done everything together, we were inseparable, and this was the only natural thing to do. I did not tell Cindy, however, that she was going to die. I just could not do that. I did not want to break her spirit, a decision that later on caused me tremendous grief, but I will discuss this later.

The days went on. Happy to be with one another, trying to get Cindy's strength back, but this approach was not working. She spent nearly all her days and nights in her new hospital bed in the living room. Bathroom breaks got more and more scary. We had a commode right beside her bed, but she was so weak I had to (using a bear hug) lift her up as she had little if any strength. I am a very strong 300+ lb person, but it took all the strength I could get together to lift her out of bed and to the commode right beside. Each time I prayed for God to give me strength and that my back would not go out as I was afraid we would both end up on the floor. One particular evening, as I lifted Cindy, her back popped and scared us both. That was it, no more getting out of bed. It was too dangerous. Thank goodness the Hospice nurse had ordered a bigger/wider hospital bed and it arrived the next morning. With it we could use a bedpan and they installed a catheter. This new bed was wonderful and made Cindy much more comfortable and safer.

6

"She's Going to Die"

It had been about a week since my heartbreaking discussion with the Hospice nurse and the reality that my dear Cynthia was indeed going to die. After fighting all the battles, endless doctor and hospital visits, pushing to get information.... she's going to die.... . No, it cannot be. She's only 54, she just became the gram'ma she dreamed of. Dear sweet babies to call her "Nanny". We have so much we want to do, trips to take, dreams to experience, plans for growing old together. Oh God, no ... it cannot be.

I cannot tell Cindy she's going to die. I cannot break her spirit. I just "cannot" do it, but what do I do? God help me to do the right thing, whatever that may be. Well, all I knew to do was tell the kids, our dear friends, and our loving minister couple. God was giving us some time to say goodbye, so that is what must be done.

I vowed not to tell Cindy what was happening and all were informed of the same. Andy and family came home from Massachusetts again. He was just starting a new job and traveling with a young baby was quite a struggle. The rest of the kids lived nearby and were able to visit as much as they wanted. Cindy's childhood friend, Lynn, lived a few hours away and so made a couple of weekend visits. Cindy was so glad to see her and the visits always brought a smile to her face. They would visit, and while Cindy slept, Lynn and I had long conversations about what was to come. She is a counselor by profession and what a help and strength she was to me. Still to this day, she is helping me grieve as she herself is, losing her life-long buddy.

As word spread through our small town, more and more friends came to visit. I made sure that they would each have their time alone with Cindy. It was hard for them, trying to carry on friendly conversation, tell old stories and laughing, all the while knowing that may be the last time they would speak. Cindy never seemed to catch on to the fact that she was going to die. During one visit with a close friend, whose daughter was going to marry in a few months, Cindy told her they she was going to have to get better so we could all go to the wedding, and was quite adamant about it.

Frequent visits were also provided by our husband—wife minister couple. Cindy had been on the search committee, that after 2 ½ years of work, found this wonderful couple. She loved both of them dearly and rightly so. Such gentle and loving souls, they brought new hope and faith into our church that was in such need. They were always ready to make a visit, say a prayer, share a laugh, or provide comfort. I do not know what our entire family would have done without them. One of the last stories about Cindy that we all love to share, occurred during a visit of our clergy couple. Cindy had not been able to attend church for nearly a year. She normally sang in the choir and was quite active in all activities. Well, during their visit, Cindy asked Laurie how the people of the church were treating her and Roger. Laurie smiled and said "just fine", to which Cindy immediately responded "well.... they better!!!"

I tried to keep things at the house as upbeat as possible. The Hospice staff came daily and helped with Cindy's care. Still wanting to be presentable, there were daily baths, clean gowns, etc. and a high school friend of Cindy's who is a beautician, came to the house and cut her hair. Such an ordeal for Cindy, having to use a lift to get out of bed and be moved to a chair, but bless her heart, she put up with it. To add more drama to the situation, a power transformer outside our house started acting up and kicked out several time. This was particularly disturbing in that we then had no air conditioning, the oxygen machine would quit, and Cindy's bed, which had an inflatable mattress, immediately would go flat. Normally, the power company was good about getting the electricity going quickly.

Then came the day that the transformer completely blew up. We waited, and waited ... no repairmen. The house was getting hotter by the minute, being July, and Cindy's deflated bed was getting quite uncomfortable. We had to do something, so I called the ambulance to come take Cindy to the emergency room and wait till we had power again. This is a day I shall forever remember. With our frequent trips to the ER, we were friends with all the nurses and felt comfortable with them. On the weekends, however, many times the attending doctor would be from out of town. All knew we were there just to wait and Cindy did not need any medical attention, but the doctor could just not stop himself from checking her out. I went along with it, thinking "ok, what ever" if you must. Then this doctor of middle eastern decent, stood by her bed and said to me in a very loud voice, "so, your wife is a terminal liver patient ... is that right?". I could have killed him on the spot. How unprofessional and heartless. I immediately got him out of the room, but I know Cindy heard what he said. To her dying day, she never mentioned a word of what the doctor had said, but somehow, she was different. That bastard.... how could he have been so stupid and unprofessional; still I must wonder if this was God's way of telling Cindy she was going to die, without any of us having to break the news to her ... I wonder.

Well, we went on with our daily routine as best we could. Many visitors and such, but the nights, it was just Cindy and I. She slept in her hospital bed in the living room, and I either on the couch or the recliner beside her. More and more, she would sleep, as I sat beside her and held her hand for hours. What a precious time it was. A time to reflect, to pray, to cry, and just somehow try to savor every moment together.

I began watching Cindy, so intently at night. One night she would sleep sound, exhausted, and then the next evening, would spend hours just looking up at the ceiling. Her eyes would move from side to side as if she was focusing in on something or someone. I would often ask her what she saw. With Cindy not being able to talk much anymore, I would say "do you see an angel, do you see someone you know?" and she would just shake her head "no", but it was obvious she was seeing something.

Watching her reminded me of a wonderful story she told me about her father who died about 18 years earlier of post-polio syndrome. One night she was with him and they all thought it was his last night, but then he made a recovery and did not pass. A few evenings later, Cindy was alone in the hospital room and said, "Dad, the other night the doctors all thought you were going to die." He then told her, "I knew I wasn't.... . the angels weren't there." Later that night, Cindy's Dad started getting worse again, said to her "the angels are here" and passed a few hours later.

A similar story involved Cindy's mother, the best mother-in-law I could have ever had. It was about eight years after Cindy's father had passed, and Mary Ann was battling cancer for the third time. She had chosen not to do any chemo, etc. this time and was letting the cancer run its course. She was in a local nursing home being cared for by Hospice. About a week before she passed, Cindy went to see her, and as she went in the room she said "Mom, how are you doing?" Mary Ann quickly replied, well I am practicing flying.... And I am pretty good at it." A bit of a chuckle, but made us wonder, was she really?? About the third day before she passed, Mary Ann went into a coma, unable to communicate and just mumbling what seemed to be non-sense. Then, out of nowhere one evening, Cindy's mother clearly said, "My name is Mary Ann". Within the hour, she had passed.

These are the things that kept running through my mind as I watched Cindy looking up at something I could not see. I kept wondering what glorious things is she seeing? Is she seeing angels, does she see her mother, does she see the face of God, what is it that she sees? I shall never forget that experience.

Daytime was frantic for me at times. Needing to run errands, go to the grocery, etc., I had the help of many friends who eagerly volunteered to do the errands. I myself was afraid to leave the house. I had to be there if Cindy needed me and how could I ever live with myself if she passed while I was shopping. The Hospice nurses told me to get out of the house for a while just to get away from everything, briefly. I understood what they were trying to do, but I just could not do that, I could not leave Cindy!!!

7

"The Final Night"

Each day after the Hospice nurse would check Cindy over, she would go in the other room with me, and anyone else that was there to give us an update on Cindy's condition. Each day would bring on more and more signs that the end was coming. I ask how Cindy would die and she told me that usually with conditions such as her's, one by one her vital systems would begin to shut down, her kidneys would stop, then her lungs would fill with fluid, and … she would literally drown. The nurse warned me that when the lungs would start filling, the sound caused by Cindy's breathing would not be pleasant.

It was July 14 and things we not going well for Cindy. Her kidney output was practically nil and she had neither eaten or drunk anything for a few days. In the early evening, Cindy became very restless, so we called the Hospice nurse for help. She told us what to do and said she would be right there.

The Hospice nurse arrived within half an hour, and after a quick check, confirmed that things were starting to shut down. Some of the kids were at the house already and the others were quickly summoned. The nurse took us all in the other room and explained what was going to transpire. She would be administering medication as quickly as she could, but there were restrictions, of which we all understood. Shortly there after, one of Cindy's dearest friends, Brenda, arrived. She had been in another town with her family, when she said for some reason she could not get her breath. She immediately left her family and hurried back to Paris knowing something was wrong with Cindy.

It was now about 6:00 PM. We all gathered around Cindy's bed and waited. The evening was one of continual prayer. Cindy had instilled deep faith in all of us and so one by one we would pray out loud. Cindy could not speak and we were not sure she could hear us, but we all prayed, and prayed, and prayed. We each spoke to her, letting her know it was OK for her to go, as hard as it was to say, but we did not want her to suffer.

At times, Cindy would open her eyes and look far above, as the Hospice nurse would explain that "she is looking far beyond here in this room". Many tears were shed, but watching the events of the evening, we all in our hearts knew she was going to a better place and were happy for her. There were times when it looked as if she was ready to pass, but she did not.

Periodically we would take a break and move to the family room, with someone staying with her. The evening seemed to go on forever. Around 8:00 PM a dear friend who is a caterer came by with a tremendous amount of food for us. She did not know Cindy was passing, but I know that God must have been involved, as He was in so many things that night.

With it appearing that the night was to be long, we each took turns sitting with Cindy, giving each time alone to reflect, pray, and continue to assure her that it was OK for her to go home to God. The nurse continued to administer medication, to calm Cindy, checking her lungs, etc. Then, it started.....". Cindy's lungs began to fill with fluid. First one lung, then the second.

Cindy's oldest son was attending Massachusetts Medical School and asked the nurse if he could use her stethoscope to listen to her lungs and did so periodically as did the nurse. From the sounds our dear Cindy was making, you could tell that the fluid retention was progressing. I will never forget one of the last times Andy checked her lungs and began to weep. Later I ask him what he heard and he said "nothing, the lung was completely full". After that, the progression sped up with the sounds getting more vivid. Once, as we all sat around the bed, the sounds became terrible and Jon, Cindy's youngest, cried out "Oh my God!!!" weeping terribly. The nurse was able to get Cindy calmed down, but what a horrific moment.

Midnight approached and Cindy was still hanging on. The Hospice nurse said she was hanging on for some reason, as she thought she was going to pass many times before, but did not. The kids decided to go home and come back in the morning. All that remained for the evening were Andy and his wife (who were staying at the house), the Hospice nurse, and myself.

The evening continued on quietly, calmly, attending to Cindy best we could. Her lungs continued to fill and Cindy "still" hanging on. Praying continued, at times thinking I have prayed all I know to pray, but we had to continue. I must admit, in the later stages of her struggle, you just wish they could give Cindy a shot to end this awful ordeal, full knowing that it is not possible or right. Still, all things run through your mind as you watch your loved one lay there and suffer.

I had gone into the kitchen to talk to the Hospice nurse on one occasion and we began a conversation about praying for miracles. Cindy had always taught me that we should not pray for what we want, but rather pray for "God's will". Previously we had dear friends come to the house and pray for a miracle. While I so appreciated their prayers, I somehow felt this was wrong by not praying for God's will. Then one of the most enlightening things of this terrible journey was given me as the Hospice nurse calmly said to me, "Greg, she is getting a miracle, she's going to heaven". How could I be so blind, not to get this, so simple, and so right.

We had gotten into the early hours of the morning. Cindy's lungs were completely filled, but bless her heart, she still was hanging on. We had all told her so many times it was okay to go and so many times she would look up far above, but she just did not want to go. Then the sun began to rise and I began to worry. Cindy's youngest son said he would be back early in the morning. Previously, he had been so upset from the terrible sounds he heard, that I said, "Cindy, its time to go now, we can't let Jon see you like this anymore". Being the protective mother till the very end, Cindy passed a few moments later. She had gone home.... It was over.

We called all the kids and Cindy's friend that had been here earlier. We covered Cindy with her mother's quilt and waited for everyone to arrive. Oh, how we all cried. Cried that our dear Cindy was not here on earth with us and cried with joy in our hearts that she was in heaven, with her Mother and all that had passed previously.

Our dear friends at the funeral home came and took Cindy's body away. Cindy's terrible 2 year fight was over. It was over.

8

"The Funeral"

Cindy passed on Friday morning. In order to notify everyone we were not able to have the visitation until the following Tuesday and the funeral on Wednesday. The days preceding the funeral were filled with making plans for the visitation at the funeral home, getting a plot at the cemetery, making plans for the funeral at our church, and notifying family. Our minister couple were such support during this time as were the entire congregation and our dear friends.

Cindy was known in Paris as the "flower lady", since she had been a floral designer for over 20 years, having a tremendous love of gardening, and possessing unparalled creativity with floral and interior design, we decided to make her visitation a tribute to her in flowers. We wanted to fill the funeral home with flowers and how our dear friends stepped up to the task.

The evening of the visitation, the family arrived early for a private viewing. I cannot tell you how magical it was walking into the funeral home. "Everywhere" we looked, there were flowers … everywhere. Flowers in the entry way, in the waiting line, in the viewing room … the entire funeral home was full to the brim with flowers. "Oh, honey see what your friends have done", I thought. Cindy looked absolutely beautiful. A week before her passing, she was terrible swollen and distended with fluid buildup, but God laid his hands on Cindy and the fluid passed out her last week with us. For the first time in months, she looked like the beautiful Cindy we all knew.

The visitation started and oh, how the people came. I cried through much of it, but I did not care. So many came to say goodbye to their dear Cindy, crying as well, but also sharing stories of how Cindy had touched their lives .. so many lives. We left the funeral home exhausted, while feeling not alone in our sorrow, as so many had come.

Wednesday morning came…. funeral day. We arrived at the church gathering in a room close to the sanctuary to await the service. A few years earlier, Cindy and I lost a very special friend, our dear Emma, whose service at this same church

23

had been glorious. With that in mind, I requested the same format for Cindy's service. The family was led into the sanctuary that was filled to capacity with friends. Special music, we had selected, was playing, as we sat there, Brenda on my left, Lynn on my right, and the rest of the family. The first selection was "It's A Wonderful World", Cindy's father's favorite song and played at his funeral. Then, "The Rose", Cindy's mother's favorite song and played at her funeral, and last "Heaven Help Me If I Ever Lose Your Love", my personal tribute to Cindy.

The service then began. Our ministers said a few opening words and declared that this service was to be a "celebration of Cindy's life". Cindy was quite involved in the church since her youth in all aspects. After our marriage, she had me join her in the choir. We both so loved music and she had such a beautiful soprano voice able to hit the highest of notes strongly. Due to this, music was an important part of the service including a flute solo of "His Eye Is On The Sparrow", and the choir singing "Here I Am Lord" and our favorite, "It Is Well With My Soul".

The highlight of the service however was when four dear friends each speaking of their thoughts and memories of Cindy. What a wonderful and gracious job each did. The music, the scripture, the epitaphs, were wonderful. Still today I have friends comment how inspirational and moving the service was. Cindy was still ministering to her friends after she passed.

At the close of the service a recording of "Amazing Grace" was played on the bagpipes. I had requested the sound be turned up to "fill the church" and oh how it did. The ride to the cemetery was quiet. Cindy, always under estimating herself would say from time to time, "I don't have any friends". As I thought of all that came to the visitation and of the church being completely filled, I had to laugh, "well honey, I told you many times how silly you were, but now you know for sure, honey "you've got friends". A few days later I was looking at the sign-in book and saw that over 300 people had come to her visitation and funeral.

At the cemetery, there was a brief service and it was over. We went home to be with friends, but also went home to a house without our dear Cindy. I wondered, how would life go on? Trying to console Cindy's children who had lost there dear mother and grandmother ("Nanny"), and thinking to myself, "what shall I do"?

9

"Alone"

It was now Friday, two days after the funeral. All have gone home. I'm here at home.... alone. Just me, Prince, our 17 year old Persian cat, and Simon, our 10 year old "Fox Red" Labrador Retriever. I just want to spend a few days by myself. All I want to do is cry.

As I have stated before, I have had a lot of death in my life, but Cindy's passing has truly ripped my heart out. I thought I had got hardened through the years starting at age 5 when my brother and I awoke one morning to find our mother, dead, in the chair she was in when we went to bed the night before. Then at age 7, when my father was killed in an auto accident, on his way home to us. At the age of 9, our grandmother, who was raising us at the time, died of kidney failure. From there my brother and I went to live with our great aunt and uncle for 14 years. During this 14 year period, my other grandparents passed. A few years later our great aunt and uncle each passed within a year of one another, then later, our Uncle (our Dad's brother) passed. Death, it was just a part of life. I would shed a few tears, but go on with life because I thought that was the way things were to be.

Cindy's passing however, was an experience that took me, and still to this day, has taken me emotionally and spiritually to places I have never been before. Never, have I felt such love ... and loss ... never. She was, and still is, my whole life. How will I go on? We did everything together and now everywhere I look, everything I see, or touch, or speak of, reminds me of my dear Cynthia. I can't talk without saying "we" or "our house" or "she". Oh, how this is going to take some time.

While my heart is broken, I cannot help but think, as I wander around our small home, so wonderfully decorated by Cindy, just how hard her life was the past two years. I was so engrossed in caring for her, trying to make her life as happy and stress free as I could, all the while doing all we could to prepare for a liver transplant, that I just did not see it. Now, as I move from room to room, I see the handrails we had to put up in the shower, the shower chair, because she was too weak to stand to bathe. In the bedroom, our adjustable beds, that provided such comfort after some of her previous surgeries. Beside the bed, was a commode, as she had become too weak to get to the bathroom, and if she did, was too weak to stand up from the toilet without my help. In the closet, a big selection of nighties, as she was often too weak to dress. By the kitchen sink were her 23 medications that we religiously took, believing in our hearts that they would be the key to a new liver. Beside the dining room table was Cindy's walker. On good days, we could leave it behind, but on many, it was so needed to get to the van for a doctor visit. As I look at all of this, it finally hits me, just how hard her life had become. Everything, and I mean "everything" was such a struggle. God bless her, she fought so hard, but I see it now. There was no quality of life for her. God gave her such a blessing when he brought her home with him. Now, for once in such a long time, she does not hurt, she can walk, and no one will ever again hurt her dear, soft, kind heart.... never again. Thank you God ... please take care of my dear Cindy.

I spent the next week at home, alone, just reflecting on what all had happened and what a wonderful marriage Cindy and I had. Life was hard for us. Seemed like there was always some battle before us, either financially, or struggles with family, co-workers, etc., but we had each other and a love so very special. Nighttime, as it had been during the last month of Cindy's life, was very special to me. Each night, during the warm July weather, I would sit out in front of the house looking at the field across from our home and then up at the stars. The stars were so bright, I would look for hours and wonder just where my Cindy was up there, what was her life like now, who was she with? Yes, many a night I would sit and cry my heart out, but afterward, I felt better and was therapeutic for me.

There were times when I questioned my decisions concerning Cindy's last few weeks. I never told her she was going to die. So afraid it would break her spirit, I just could not do it. At the time it seemed the right thing, but now I have many regrets. Because of my decision, we never got to talk about her passing, what she felt about it, what she wanted me to do, how she wanted me to go on. Now, I will never have the answers to these questions and I feel so cheated. I must remind myself that God did give us a month at home together, such a precious gift. Cindy did not die quickly as so many of my other family member, without "any" chance to say goodbye. While I never told Cindy she was going to die, she must have known. She had to wonder why late at night I would tell her how much I loved her as tears ran down my face. She had to know.

Since Cindy's passing, a dear friend who has helped me understand much of this, shared with me some of what she went through with her own mother as she was dying of cancer. She had tried to talk to her mother about her dying, but the mother would have no part of it. She knew she was going to die and wanted to enjoy what time she had left talking about happy things and not dwell on the bad. I must think that Cindy would have been the same way.

The other thing that was causing me terrible heartbreak was that before Cindy passed, she did not tell me she loved me. I told her constantly, but she said nothing in return and that hurt me so. The reality of it is that I know without doubt that she loved me, but at that point in time, Cindy simply could not talk. Still, it lingers with me wishing to have heard those words.

My week at home alone was coming to an end. A week of contemplation, prayer, tremendous tears, and sorrow, but a journey I had to do myself. Now, it was time to return to life.

10

"I Saw A Dragonfly"

The following week I returned to work. It was good to be back with my friends at IDOT. Yes, it was hard and I spent a lot of time in my cubical alone crying, but I was back at work and getting back into life. The past 2 years had been a struggle for not only Cindy and me, but for my co-workers as well. The love and support they provided leaves me at a loss for words. I had to be gone from work so much and they all willingly chipped in to cover for me, gave encouragement, and prayed constantly for us. Such loyalty and friendship in today's world is most uncommon.

Life got into a routine again. Yes, it was different and changes made; no need to hurry home now ... not now. Then one day, it was a Thursday, the beginning of many wonderful gifts from Cindy began. I was e-mailing back and forth with Cindy's friend, Lynn. Lynn said that she had told Cindy, during one of her last visits, that she wanted her to send her a sign that she was OK and was still waiting. She just knew it was going to involve dragonflies somehow as she and Cindy both loved anything with dragonflies on it (i.e., pictures, pillows, figurines, fabric, etc.). We ended our little chat and went on about our day.

Later in the day, Lynn e-mailed me back all excited. She had just seen an old co-worker she had not seen in some time and when the lady turned to look at her, the only jewelry she had on was a big dragonfly pin. Well, Lynn "knew" this was a sign from Cindy and that she knew we were talking about her. I must admit, I thought, "yeah .. OK", if you think that OK, but I was not convinced.

Then it began. When I left the office that night I walked to the parking lot to get in our van. As I approached the van I saw something and thought, it can't be. Yes, it was a dragonfly, flying around the van. Then, when I got inside, the dragonfly hovered in front of the windshield and just looked at me. Oh my God, it was Cindy. I cannot tell you what joy overcame me. Somehow I did not feel so alone anymore.

Here I was, receiving a sign from Cindy, wanting to tell someone, but who? Who could I share this exciting news with that would not think I had lost my mind? Later that I night I decided to email Andy and tell him of the days events. Being quite a spirit-filled young man, I hoped he would believe me and share in the excitement. I waited for a response, but nothing, and I continued to wait. Then, about 2 weeks later, Andy called me to see how I was doing. He did not bring it up, so I was forced to, still full of joy from the day. I ask him if he received my email and he said he did. Then, he went on to say, "I received that e-mail on a Friday night. The next morning I was waiting on our back deck for Jennifer to come out and hold the ladder because I was going to clean the gutters of our condo. Greg, you won't believe what happened. As I sat waiting, 3 dragon-flies came and landed within 6 inches of my hand. Greg, we don't have dragon-flies out here in Massachusetts and I said out loud, Mom ... I know its you!" Then to top that off the next day Andy explained he was on the ladder on the front of their condo. His baby daughter was upstairs in her crib taking a nap, when he looked over at her window and saw 2 dragonflies hovering outside her window. Andy said he then yelled at Jennifer "honey, I know you are going to think I am crazy, but open Gabby's curtain. The dragonflies looked in for a while and then flew away. Cindy had never been strong enough to travel to Massachu-setts to see her new grandbaby in her own home, but now she could ... thank you God.

This was the beginning of the dragonfly stories that still go on today. All of Cindy's children have had multiple experiences as she had kept her presence known to us. I had ordered a few books on grieving, wanting to find some answers to "how long will this go on, is the extreme sorrow I am feeling normal, how am I to go on now, ...". When the books arrived, I was perusing through them as I had only ordered based on title and had no idea as to their content. Then all at once I could not believe what I was seeing!!! In one of the books ... the title of Chapter 6 "Dragonflies". Seems it is somewhat common for contact to be made with ones that have passed through dragonflies. You cannot imagine the astonishment I felt reading and re-reading what it said.

On another evening, I was cleaning out drawers and seeing what was in our TV cabinet. The kids had gotten us a DVD player a couple of years ago and two movies. I had forgotten about both of them, till I saw them again and you cannot believe what one of them was. The movie was "Dragonfly", with Kevin Costner. I remembered back that we had once tried to watch it, but that a man's wife dies in the beginning, upsetting Cindy, so we never watched the movie. Well, I immediately sat down and watched the movie all the way through. It was about

Kevin Costner's wife that had passed and she was using dragonflies to contact him, just as my Cindy was doing. I know in my heart that she guided me to the movie that night.

Each year in December, Cindy and I would decorate the Christmas tree at my office. She was as very talented as a decorator, that everyone eagerly awaited what she would come up with each year. This December, 5 months after her passing, I was determined to do a special tree in honor of Cindy. She had always loved trees covered with just silver and crystal. Well, I had gone to the nearby Hobby Lobby to shop for supplies. As I stood in front of the crystal ornaments, I just could not decide what to get. I said to myself "Cindy, help me out here." Then, as I looked down at the bottom of the shelf, behind a couple of ornaments, was it what I thought it was? Yes, it was a crystal dragonfly. In fact there were 6 of them stuck back on there. Of course I immediately grabbed all of them, not believing I had found them. I continued shopping and quickly all the decorations I needed fell into place. At this store, they were playing music over the intercom and I was listening to it as I shopped. Then I stopped in my tracks, was I really hearing what I thought I was? Yes, they were playing "It Is Well With My Soul", that glorious anthem that the choir had sung at Cindy's memorial service. Oh God, what a day you have given me, thank you Jesus. The dragonfly ornaments and then the music, "honey I know you're with me, thank you sweetie!"

The dragonfly stories continue to grow in number and are so very special to me. I read in one of the books I ordered that loved ones that have passed will try to send you signs to let you know they are OK, but you must be open to watching for them. I've seen them, continue to see them, and I know that Cindy's spirit is with me always. It is winter now, but I cannot wait for spring, more appropriate dragonfly weather.

Cindy's stone at the cemetery, I wanted, naturally, to be something very special. Each Memorial Day and Veteran's Day, she would make arrangements for her family members as well as mine. We would go to the cemetery together and carefully place the flowers, cleaning up the headstone, etc. Through our trips together, we would look at all the different types of stones and she took a particular liking to the newer monuments that were like garden benches. Remembering this, my choice was already made when I went to order her stone, but I really wanted to make it something special for her and once again it was obvious. With all that had happened, there had to be dragonflies on her garden bench. When the bench was done, it was just absolutely beautiful. Simple in design, but so tasteful.... just like Cindy, and on the seat of the bench was carved a big dragonfly that looked as if it just landed there. How wonderful.

Spring is coming and I cannot wait to share with friends another story about, "I Saw A Dragonfly"

11

"What Now?"

My journey now is to try to get some kind of life back in order. A life without Cindy here on earth. There never is a day that goes by without me thinking back, remembering her, shaking my head in disbelief that she is really gone. Time and time again I say it to myself that I know she is so much better off, and I truly thank God for that, but I still am in shock that she is gone. Oh how my heart hurts from missing her, but I must learn to live with that hurt. Never, do I ever want to reach a place where it does not hurt, but hope that more and more I will just smile and picture her in heaven surrounded by God's glory. That is where I want to go.

Cindy was such a special person to so many people, that as part of this closure process I wanted to do some projects to memorialize her and the love that she shared with all who knew here. I felt too, that these projects would be something tangible that I could create and enjoy for the rest of my time on this earth.

The first thing I did was to develop a PowerPoint slideshow of various pictures of Cindy, her children, and me. She had such a warm smile and a hysterical laugh, I wanted the photos to be of happy times. Cindy coveted each of her children and when the grandchildren started coming along, oh even more the glee and excitement. Watching her hold her grandbabies, you knew that for Cindy, life was complete. One particular photo I selected was of Cindy holding a sign saying "I Love You Gabby". We were never able to make the trip to Massachusetts to see this little bundle of joy when she was born, so it was our way of sending love to our precious Gabrielle via e-mail. Each photo holds such special memories; I had to find the perfect song to accompany the presentation. After much searching, I found just the song, "If I Had Only Known" recorded by Reba McEntire. It is so special, I must share the words with you:

> If I had only known, it was our last walk in the rain, I'd keep you out for hours in the storm. I would hold you hand like a lifeline to my heart. Underneath the thunder we'd be warm.

If I had only known, I'd never hear your voice again, I'd memorize each word you ever said. And on those lonely nights, I would think of them once more, and keep your words alive inside my head. If I had only known, I'd never hear your voice again.

You were the treasure in my hand. The one who always stood beside me, so unaware, I foolishly believed that you would always be there. And then there came a day, when I, turned my head, and you slipped away.

If I had only known, it was my last night by your side, I'd pray a miracle to stop the dawn. And when you'd smile at me, I would look into your eyes, and make sure you know my love for you goes on and on.

If I had only known. If I had only known. Oh, the love I would have shown.

If I had only,…. known.

This song is so beautiful and moving, it could not say any better how I feel about my life with Cindy and how I feel about things now. I encourage you to find a copy of this wonderful song a listen to it intently. The photo collage has been good for me to create as well as to utilize. I still watch it at least every other day and it makes me feel closer to Cindy.

As you know, music was a big part of Cindy's and my life. We both loved to sing in our church choir, especially during Christmas and Easter, as the anthems were always superb and so inspirational. Well, my second of three projects, was going to be giving a shot at writing a song to Cindy. I am a civil engineer, not a song writer, but felt compelled to give it a try. Surprisingly, the words and melody came together quite quickly. I feel in my heart that God was leading me through the creation of this song. The accompaniment is yet to come and will have to be done by an honest musician. My inspiration came from watching Cindy late at night during the last couple of weeks of her life. As I have said earlier, late at night she would just look up at the ceiling, scanning from side to side, looking. She could not tell me what she was seeing, though I asked, but you could tell she was seeing something. She would look and look, till she fell asleep. As time progressed, she would sleep all one night, as if resting up for a night of looking and then the following evening spend considerable time looking up, searching from side to side. I could only imagine what she was seeing, but it had to be glorious. So that was my inspiration for the following song to my dear Cynthia:

Till I See What You See

Night after night, I sit by your bed.
Hold your hand and think of all we've done.
The past 2 years, you've fought so hard,
But now my dear, he's calling you home.

Have the angels come,
Do you see the light,
Do you see the face of God?
Please tell me dear what it is,
Just what it is you see

There's a peace in the house tonight.
All have gone to bed.
Just you and I, hold'in hands, still trying to be one.
As the sun starts to rise, I can see its time to go
No turning back, he's calling you home.

Have the angels come,
Do you see the light,
Do you see the face of God?
Please tell me dear what it is,
Just what it is you see

Our Lord has promised you a miracle my dear.
The gift of eternal life, the gift to live with him.
So receive it my lovely one, lift up your hands to him.
Let him guide you home as he promised, and receive his miracle.

So goodbye my love until that day
When I'll see what you see.
Please wait for me, pray for me, till I see what you see.

My final project I wanted to complete, to bring some closure to Cindy's passing was the writing of this book for two reasons. First, I wanted to share with the world just what a true "angel on earth" Cindy was. Life was so hard for her, always fighting battles, but through it all she never lost her faith, ability to love & forgive, and touched so many lives along the way. Secondly, so many people of our small community have given so much through their love, prayers, and acts of kindness, as well as the endless blessings received from God, that I in some way wanted to give back and possibly help someone else going through the grieving process.

12

"Learning to Live Again"

As I said earlier, I am an engineer, not a songwriter or a therapist. All I can pass on is what seems to have helped me during my grieving, which still continues today. Some of the things that have helped me are:

- Talk to people about how you are feeling. Don't try to keep it in or deny that you're grieving. You have to grieve, its just a matter of when you choose to go through it and I recommend to not delay. You may have to be selective who you discuss things with, as some are reluctant, but the best is to find someone who has already grieved, via death, divorce, or some tragedy. They will know where you are coming from.

- Read some books on grieving. It will give you some perspective on what to expect, or rather "not" expect of yourself. Telling yourself to "snap out of it" is easy, but trust me, time must pass before that can happen.

- Talk to people that have grieved. While each case is different, it is valuable knowledge to know how others traveled down the path you presently are on.

- Pray, pray, pray. Pray for God to help you through this. Talk to your loved one that has passed. They may not be able to answer, but they can hear you. Give yourself time alone, time to think, time to reflect, and time to cry. Yes, that's right.... cry. There are times when all I want to do is cry, and so I give myself the time and place to do so. Just let it all out. I can't tell you how much better you will feel..... it really does help.

- Don't be surprised at the wide array of thoughts that you will have. My mind has gone everywhere. They may seem silly at the time, but are indeed legitimate thoughts. For instance, one day I was at the cemetery, talking to Cindy and reflecting. We had always dreamed that when I retired from my current job, that we would move to the panhandle of Florida, an area we fell in love with, and I would get a job down there. Thinking of this, I first thought, "well

36

guess its time to get your resume ready", then it hit me. There is "no way" I could leave Paris now. I can't leave Cindy and I could not come to see her here at the cemetery. Logic told me that she would be with me in spirit where ever I was, but my heart told me no. Later, I was sharing, what I thought were irrational feelings, with a close friend who had lost her husband, and she told me she felt the very same way. It's good to talk to friends about "everything", for you will find that your feelings are real, valid, and not uncommon.

- Recently I listened to a radio program featuring a woman that was grieving from the loss of her husband. She so eloquently discussed what she was going through and spoke exactly of what I was feeling. One of her best analogies was, "it is like there is a knife in my heart all the time and every once in a while someone, or something, will bump it, bringing back all the hurt". Time however seems to lessen the frequency of these events, but they will always occur.

- Some advice to friends of the grieving. Let them talk and encourage them to do so. Your job however, should be to listen, just listen. Too often people try to validate a conversation by saying something like, "yes, but the time you had together was so special". While that may be true, the griever does not need to hear that yet. All they know is their heart is broken and they are trying to get someone to see that. Help them by listening and validating "their" feelings.

I hope that some of this has been of help to you in your grieving, or at least given you some possible direction in your changed life. For me, I don't know when or if my sorrow will ever ease, but I must keep trying to live. God gave Cindy the gift of eternal life, surpassing anything I ever could or ever had wanted to give her. She is living in His glory now. She doesn't hurt anymore and no one will "ever" again hurt her soft, dear heart. The only thing now is my own selfish grief. I talk to her all the time, cry when I need to, and thank God for taking care of my dear Cynthia.

I find, I don't know how to pray these days. Before, all my prayers were centered around Cindy, but struggle now on what to say. I know she is OK and with the best caregiver of all times. My prayers now, while difficult, are for God to give me guidance and direction. I need to know what path he now wants me to follow and what work he wants me to do, so for now I pray and listen.... listen for his direction.

I am now living each day as it comes, realizing some will be better than others, but that is OK. My faith is stronger than ever. Without it, I would be very bitter, but I know for sure where Cindy is and who all she is with. Thank you God for taking care of my dear Cynthia, and until that day when I am with her again, I shall continue to look each day..... . for another dragonfly.

God Bless You All

13

Epitaphs From Cindy's Memorial Service and Exerts from Special E-mails and Letters

Cindy, Working in the Lord's Garden—John Robson

Some of us here were participants in the Disciple program that Elizabeth led some years back. I know that Cindy and Greg were among those that faithfully gathered each Sunday for 32 weeks (can you believe). We altered our meeting locale when Cindy had knee surgery, but we never thought of not meeting. Cindy was not the official teacher but she was the center of our communal prayer life.

One passage we studied at length summarizes what we aspired to and what we continue to aspire for. Perhaps knowing and loving Cindy has given me resolve because she had already taken prayer into her very substance and wanted the same for all of us. And she loved all with a fierce love that knew no bounds—love for those who were close and love for those unknown in need of love.

It is these verses that most speak to me about my friend Cindy.

Listen to these words from Romans 12, beginning at verse 9. I want us all to think of how these words capture how each of our lives was touched and entwined by Cindy and her love.

Love

Romans 12:9-18,21
Love must be sincere.
Hate what is evil; cling to what is good.
Be devoted to one another in brotherly love.
Honor one another above yourselves.
Never be lacking in zeal, but keep your spiritual fervor, serving the Lord.
Be joyful in hope, patient in affliction, faithful in prayer.
Share with God's people who are in need.
Practice hospitality.

Bless those who persecute you; bless and do not curse.

Rejoice with those who rejoice; mourn with those who mourn.

Live in harmony with one another.

Do not be proud, but be willing to associate with people of low position.

Do not be conceited.

Do not repay anyone evil for evil.

Be careful to do what is right in the eyes of everybody.

If it is possible, as far as it depends on you, live at peace with everyone..... [as it says in Proverbs}
"If your enemy is hungry, feed him; if he is thirsty, give him something to drink. In doing this, you will heap burning coals on his head."

Do not be overcome by evil, but overcome evil with good.
    I think in terms of analogies. Jesus used them frequently so that mortals might grasp the truth. When I think of Cindy, I think of her has a gardener in the fields of her Savior, Jesus Christ.
    She is know to all as the flower lady, one who could garden with the best, perhaps learned from her mom. Both were ladies with attitude with a capital A. Cindy could turn the common plants and grasses into a refuge of beauty, both on

her own turf and yours if you so wished. And when she could no longer turn the earth, she could inspire others—chiefly Greg—to do it and inspire others that it would turn out not just fine, but beautiful.

In this church of her childhood, where once upon a time she was baptized at this very font and where she once stood in starched choir robe as a member of the cherub choir, Cindy took up her task as a gardener.

Others can speak to her music and role in the choir. But here she gardened too with voice lifted up to the glory of God. And many of us know how dear to heart were such songs as Sweet Little Jesus Boy.

And I could not begin to speak of her role as mother. Others here have that exclusive right.

And nor can I speak of her role as wife and all that unfolds in the boundaries of a marriage blessed by God.

But I can speak as a congregant whom she befriended and enlisted in the work at hand.

It was in Vacation Bible School not so many years ago. Presbyterians had not hosted one on their own for a number of years and no volunteers were fighting to provide leadership. And then there was Cindy, who always believed in planting seeds and nurturing young plants, in this instance the children of Paris. She assumed the mantel and we all got in line, if with some reservations. The old questions arose. Were we too small? Should we hook up with the Disciples or Methodists? She said we can do it and we should pray each day. Pray that there would be enough volunteers, pray that there would be enough resolve, and pray for the kids to come—any kids. Elizabeth and I were new at this and lacking in self-confidence. But she—as an agent of God, I do believe—imparted confidence. We can do our job and the kids will come. In the end, we had 60 kids. We were tired each day and yet came back the next. And no one was more tired than she. But she knew God put her in this leadership job and failure was not possible.

Then there was the job of deacon and more opportunity to tend the garden of the Lord. She was the chairman, though all too willing for others to step forward. She always saw herself in terms of modesty and surely others were better equipped, she thought. But into the leadership void she stepped and lured me in to my inaugural journey as a deacon. She paid scant attention to the adopted budget or past tradition. The Deacons would strive to minister to all, not just the worthy poor (and there was some talk of who was making an effort and deserving of our help). She knew from life that sometimes a mother may screw up but still needed if not deserved a helping hand with putting food on the table. She introduced me to families in Paris with floors of dirt. How could that be, I would ask.

She would not share all she knew from a lifetime of residency, just told me we have to help. And in the midst of this serious work she would always find something that would bring laughter, even while confronting our serious work. For Cindy understood that laughter was a gift of God to be used in the garden. The foibles of pastors often provided gist for well-intentioned humor. I will never forget sitting in the parlor to the side awaiting our chance on the Session Agenda to make a case for more money. We got to laughing a bit too much, causing Carolyn Hodge to shush us for disrupting business. But I digress.

As mentioned above, Cindy was one to invite all in to work in the garden. Few here avoided her sweet (or at time not quite so sweet) telephone call to help out in some project. Which is why I stand here today. Cindy talked with me about teaching Junior High. She knew little of me really and perhaps really wished that Larry or Fred would transfer their own Church work detail to take the class that all were more than a bit leery of. She told me that the need was there and "I would be so good." How many of you can still hear those words tripping off her lips. Could you say no? So I enlisted in the ranks of Sunday School teachers, learning then as now as much and more from the kids as I have to teach them. Cindy hooked me for life seemingly as a junior gardener working in the garden with the young seedlings.

And now I must speak on behalf of the Robson family in what to each of the three of us was one of the most magnanimous statements of hospitality, as mentioned in Romans, and inclusion.

Some years back, none of us knows the year [1994 is what V says], we got a call from Cindy. She asked if we would be going to Christmas Eve services at church—something so dear to her heart. I said yes. Well, she asked, would we like to come over for a simple supper before? We said yes. It seemed like a wonderful invite—the three of us, such a small family, being invited to partake of the Christmas spirit with her family, including mom and brother, son-in-law, plus any steady girlfriends of the day. Dinner was endless laughs after first we gathered in an extended circle for Andy to lead us in prayer. We had poppers, funny hats, and could hear Uncle Tim regaling the 'children's table' with stories.

At the end of dinner, we were told that gifts in their family were chiefly opened on Christmas Eve. We thought to excuse ourselves, promising to meet up at church later that night.

But not so. The Robsons were to be a part of the gifting, and not just from Cindy and Greg. We found that she had asked her family to widen the circle and include the Robsons. We were a bit shocked and very humbled. We had never expected such expressions of Christmas love. Victoria, I recall, was particularly amazed. We had brought no gifts and here we were receiving so much.

This became a yearly tradition, one not taken lightly ever. Rarely have we been the beneficiary of such abundant and unexpected love.

We were not singled out for this love. I know that all of you here have your on examples of Cindy's love flowing freely over you when you least expected it—like God's Grace it came unearned—but when you were most in need.

We are privileged to call her friend and marvel that God raised up such a woman of faith and love, or grace and beauty. The best way to honor her will be to take the verses of Roman 12 and make them a part of our everyday fiber as she certainly did.

I conclude with a poem that Cindy commented upon when Glenna Kreckman read it from the pulpit one Memorial Sunday the year Lloyd O'Bannon joined the cavalcade of saints and left us.

Crossing the Bar—Alfred, Lord Tennyson

Sunset and evening star,
And one clear call for me!
And may there be no moaning of the bar,
When I put out to sea,
But such a tide as moving seems asleep,
Too full for sound and foam,
When that which drew from out the boundless deep
Turns again home.

Twilight and evening bell,
And after that the dark!
And may there be no sadness of farewell,
When I embark;
For tho' from out our bourne of Time and Place
The flood may bear me far,
I hope to see my Pilot face to face
When I have crost the bar.

"I'd like to say a few words about my best buddy Cindy."

A Celebration Of Cindy by Lynn Adams McCann

When Greg and I first discussed my speaking at Cindy's service as a tribute to her life, my immediate reaction was "Why of course", but then it dawned on me.... I'm not a speaker, I'm not a writer, and for sure I am not a storyteller, but there is one thing I am certain of is that I am a very private person. Cindy knew this best about me. What on earth was I thinking??.... Because it is such an emotional time, I wasn't even certain if I could utter one word.

I won't be sharing any Cindy & Lynn stories with you today, but I am here to tell you that Cindy and I had something very unusual and unique ... it is something that is growing ever increasingly extinct and that is.... a beautiful "LIFE-LONG FRIENDSHIP". Our friendship began at age 3 and spanned over 52 years. When I told this to someone the other day, they said to me...."that is unheard of in this day and age"! And sadly, I began thinking of how much truth was in that statement.... .thinking of how much we all definitely live in a very fast paced world and a world of Technology.... it seems to me that we have replaced best friends and family with ... Laptops, E-mails, Faxes, Game Boys, Cell phones, Blackberry's, MP3's, and I Pod's and on and on.

What I'd like to say ... is not to surround your life totally with these gadgets, but rather take time out to surround yourself with your best friend as well as your family members. Because in the end, Friends are what matter the most ... the years, the tears, the smiles and the laughter shared. I am thankful for the opportunity to experience a friendship like Cindy's and mine that endured the trials and tribulations throughout the 52 very short years. Cindy was the most kind, most generous, most beautiful, upbeat fun-loving person I have ever known. She was such a dear friend and buddy, I will miss her tremendously.

Thank-you Cindy.

TRIBUTE TO CINDY IDLEMAN
With love from Jane Blair 7-19-06

I remember when Cindy's mother Mary Ann was dying of cancer, they made a pact to "meet each other by the river" in heaven. This was a testament to their assurance through Christ that death would not separate them and they would meet again in heaven. We take comfort in that same assurance, knowing Cindy is now rejoicing at heaven's river with her Mother and Father and her precious Savior. The choir will soon sing a favorite hymn that Cindy and Greg have sung with us and that has a special message of comfort. It begins,

"When peace, like a river, attends my way, When sorrows like sea billows roll—Whatever my lot, Thou has taught me to say, 'It is well, it is well with my soul.'"

Cindy lived her life with that same peace which is like a river. It grew from her deep faith in Christ and flowed throughout her being. With that in mind, let's explore the metaphor of the river and how it relates to Cindy's life. (As I do so, please remember that I have just an elementary understanding of the geology of rivers.)

First, a river has an origin, often in mountain streams filled by rains and melting snow. These small streams rush quickly and make their way through rocky terrain, changing direction many times and eventually straightening out and carving a valley. I remember Cindy as a girl (not too much younger than I, mind you), radiating vitality and vivaciousness, and like that mountain stream, plunging headlong into life. Freida Witters recently shared a sweet story about Cindy that illustrates her spunk and spirit. When Freida was expecting one of her children, Mary Ann and young Cindy (who lived nearby) saw her outside one day. Cindy rushed up to Freida and, pulling up her maternity top and poking her expanded tummy, asked insistently, "What's in there?" Yes, we loved Cindy for her spirited approach to life. As for the rocky terrain and the twists and turns of life, Cindy had her share of hardships—her father's polio, Andy's eye problem as a baby when Cindy was such a young mother, her difficulties as a single mother of four. Throughout it all she relied on her faith and her mother's encouraging support.

And then God brought her Greg. Like two tributaries that flow together to make a river, their union made each of them stronger and more complete. Mary Ann, in her customary spirit of thankfulness, declared that Greg was the answer to her prayers for Cindy, and oh, how he has been that! Greg, you have been

Cindy's soul mate and steady support, and she knew she could always count on you, especially the past two years. Your love enabled her river of life to flow in a more strong and sure way than it could have alone.

Cindy's river was not a shallow one. She had great depth of faith and a spirituality that I feel privileged to have shared. Cindy and I served together in many aspects of church life: mainly choir, Christian education, Deacons, and the PNC. She often sat by me in choir, and I loved to hear her clear and beautiful natural soprano voice as she belted out those high notes I could never hope to reach! A number of years ago Cindy brought new life to our Vacation Bible School when she served as director. Her first year we started the week with a dozen or so children, doubled that number the next day and had close to 60 children in attendance by week's end—primarily due to Cindy's efforts, energy, and enthusiasm. And such fun we all had—children and adults alike—performing Bible School songs, complete with motions, in front of the congregation during the worship service! Cindy also set a new standard when she served as a Deacon. She launched several new programs, and she had a knack for finding families in need and leading the way in serving others with the biggest and most caring heart I've ever known. Most recently, Cindy and I served together on the Pastoral Nominating Committee that brought Rodger and Laurie to us. It was a long and sometimes difficult process, but largely because Cindy was with us, it also became a faith journey that helped us grow spiritually. When we would be down and dispirited, Cindy would find just the right words—usually in prayer—to lift us up and keep us positive. She always reminded us that God was at work in our lives, but on His timetable, not ours. (She was right, as Rodger and Laurie have been a blessing to us all.) Cindy was also our "Paris ambassador," and as a realtor, she knew all the locations and everything about our community to share with and impress prospective pastors. (We called it the "dime" tour—much better than the normal "nickel" tour most people would give.) Yes, Cindy lived her faith and cared deeply for Christ and all of God's children.

We can't forget the plants and flowers that adorn a riverbank and bring it beauty and color. Some people love flowers. Cindy LOVED flowers! I was always impressed by her knowledge of all the flowers' names and the best locations for them to flourish and enhance their surroundings, and her natural eye for arranging flowers artistically. She probably couldn't count how many floral arrangements, bouquets, and corsages she created for people over the years. In years past she loved working with Brenda Wright in decorating for weddings and transforming the KC Hall into something magical and beautiful for the annual hospital gala. Yes, Cindy was the "flower lady" to us all.

Similar to the plant life along a river are the fish and other creatures spawned within the river. For Cindy, these were her precious children and grandchildren. Drew was an unexpected blessing—their "miracle baby." Sadly, she had become ill by the time Gabby and Grace were born, but that did not diminish her pleasure in having granddaughters, and all three grandchildren brought her overflowing joy and delight.

As a river ages, its floodplain widens and the river becomes more visible for miles around. Likewise, Cindy came to be known to many people in many different capacities. All of you here today, and those who came to the funeral home yesterday evening, are a testament to how widely she was known and loved. Each one of us will cherish in our hearts special memories of Cindy, both happy and sad. Ever since her passing, I've felt her presence around and within me in a very palpable and powerful way, and I know that, while she may be gone from us physically, she's definitely still with us in spirit … and always will be.

Finally, the river comes to its end. But it doesn't end! Rather, it flows into the sea and takes on new life as part of a larger body of water. Cindy's life here on earth may have ended, but her journey has taken on a new and perfect life in heaven, her soul at peace with God.

I'll close with a promise similar to the one Cindy shared with her mother. Remember the "Billy Bass" on a plaque that was popular a few years back and the song he belted out with irritating repetition? ("Take me to the river; throw me in the water.") With apologies to you all, this is to my dear Cindy:

"I'll meet you by the river, and we'll sing Hallelujah!"

Praise God … I love you, Cindy!

E-mail From Greg Idleman to Family & Friends 1 Week After Cindy's Passing:
Sent: Friday, July 21, 2006 12:01 AM
Subject: Thank You

Well, it's all over now. Andy and his family flew back to Boston this morning. Quiet here in the house, which is good and bad. Each of you have provided such love and support that any words I may find seem so inadequate. Your cards, visits, and prayers while Cindy was still able to converse meant so much. So many prayers, acts of kindness, willingness to do anything, were endless.

A tremendous thank you to all who participated in the service at the church. It indeed surpassed any conceivable expectations.

Over 300 people came to her visitation. As we pulled away from the church on our way to the cemetery I thought of that and all that were able to attend the funeral, it made me laugh…. in Cindy's usual manner of underestimating herself and her effect on people she would say to me "I don't have any friends". I would always tell her how ridiculous she was, but the showing of love you all gave, indeed proved her wrong.

While my heart is broken, I cannot help but smile that she no longer hurts and rid of her worn out body. As you know, I have experienced many deaths in my life, but this one is REALLY hurting. No one "ever" loved me as she did. It is going to take some time…. going to take some time.

Thank you all for your love … thank you, thank you. We were all "touched by an angel" and her name was Cindy.

Greg

E-mail From Greg Idleman to Insurance Company Nurse—Case Worker:

Received your lovely card and so I know you have learned of Cindy's passing. You are such a special person that I cannot begin to thank you for all that you have done through this terrible struggle. When we returned home from the hospital the last time, I thought we had just a huge setback, but we were both committed to overcoming it. Quickly though, it became obvious that it was not to be.

Thank you so for getting us signed up with Hospice. What a wonderful gift you gave Cindy and I. They were truly superb in all ways and allowed Cindy to pass in her own home with dignity and grace.... thank you. You have no idea how important that was. The last several hours that Cindy was with us, her kidneys shut down and then the lungs began filling with fluid. The Hospice nurse spent the entire time with us and what a God send. I do not know what we would have done without her. All of Cindy's children were here and what could have been a horrible situation was kept well under control through the nurse's constant monitoring and administering of medication to keep her calm. While her death was vivid, it was graceful.

At 5:30 AM Saturday morning, the sun started to rise. It was just Cindy, myself, Andy (Cindy's oldest son), and the nurse. The rest of the children had gone to their homes with a promise to return early. During the evening, in one episode, the fluid in her lungs was making that awful sound and was more than her youngest son could take, upsetting him terribly. As the son arose, I began worrying that he would return. I talked to Cindy and said, "Honey, we can't let Jon see you like this again, it is time to go". The loving, protective mother was still there in her last moments and she passed shortly there after.

Cindy was the spiritual foundation of the family and she showed us the gift of God's love each day. While we miss her terribly, we know she is with the Lord and praise in his glory. She no longer hurts, she no longer cries to see her mother, they are all together now. She showed me what it is to truly be loved and I will hold that to my heart.

I was going to call and say these things, but all I am able to do now is smile and cry at the same time. I wish you could have met her in person; she was indeed an angel.

Thank you again from the bottom of my heart. This seems so inadequate, but all I can do. I will be in touch as I do need to get serious about the by-pass surgery or j-band. I have gained so much weight through all of this, I must do something. If you would, please pass this on to your supervisor. I want everyone in your organization to know what you have done for us and what a kind and loving person you are.

Thank you and Praise God!!!

Greg Idleman

Email from Greg Idleman to Church Ministers, 1 month after Cindy's passing:

Just wanted to let you know how nice your church service was today and thank you for remembering Cindy. I hesitated coming as I knew I would just sit there and cry.... and I did.... oh well, what the heck. I keep waiting for the tears to pass so I can come back, but today proved it is going to be a while. I know Cindy was with us today. I was sitting there not even thinking of her and was overcome by emotion.

Thank you all. You have made this horrible time much easier. Elation for where Cindy is, horrible for my own selfish grief.

Thank you.
Gregory L. Idleman

2006 Christmas Letter:
Christmas 2006

Well as you all know it's been quite a year. One full of sadness and yet a chance for all of us to reflect and think about what truly is "important" in life. Yes, our dear Cindy is no longer here on earth with us, but is still a big part of our lives and there is no question where she is. Heaven now has a glorious soprano in their choir and it must be even more beautiful than ever. For me, it has been a time when my faith has grown to an all time high. While sad, life now makes sense somehow, and holds wonderful things to come, even in passing. I have thanked each of you before, but want to one last time. It has overwhelmed me of the absolutely tremendous outpour of sincere acts of kindness, prayers, and words of encouragement when so needed. Thank you all, from the bottom of my heart.... Thank You.

Christmas is a time of joy and we are going to make it that. Andy and family were able to make it home for Thanksgiving. The whole gang came (Andy, Jennifer, Gabby, Ginni, Tom, Drew, Tim, Jon, Daniel, and last but not least "Gracie Bear"). We all pitched in and had a traditional Thanksgiving Dinner, which turned out great, except for the noodles. All had full tummies, so who cares. Even Simon (our 10 year old Labrador) and Princie (17 year old cat) got a special dinner.

I've started back to church and singing in the choir. Cindy and I just loved the Christmas anthems and brings back good memories. Recently sang in a community concert with all the church choirs in the Paris area. That many voices makes a wonderful sound. Amazing the talent in our small community. Looking forward to caroling with our church choir. Such a wonderful way to spread the Christmas spirit. I vividly remember when they came to our home last year and sang to Cindy and I. How wonderful it felt to be included. So, if you get the chance to help out with caroling, a charity, food pantry, etc. please do. Makes you feel better about yourself, spreads God's love, and certainly will bring a smile to those receiving the gift.

Christmas Eve I am having the kids and a few close friends over for dinner and as every year I am sure the conversation will turn to Cindy's memorable & hilarious rendition of "Sweet Little Jesus Boy" (wish we had it on tape … it was a scream!!). Then, going to Christmas Eve service at 11:00 PM to bring in Christmas Day. This is the highlight of the season for me. A truly amazing service with the most beautiful music, what a better way to celebrate the birth of our Lord. I remember back the first year Cindy and I were married. Started to snow heavily as we went into church and when we came out there were several inches of white, fluffy snow. So, when we got home after midnight, the two of us went for a walk around the subdivision … how fun!!!

Well enough of all that. Just wanted to wish you all a wonderful Christmas. Remember what Christmas is really about. Take some time for yourselves and think about all the blessing you have. Hug the kids and grandkids. Thanks for being such wonderful friends. Love you all.

Greg Idleman "Grandy"

978-0-595-46390-1
0-595-46390-8